Mallet Eyes

MALLET EYES

Poems by

Jeremy Sigler

Left Hand Books

Copyright © 2000 by Jeremy Sigler. All rights reserved.

The publisher gratefully acknowledges the John W. and Clara C. Higgins Foundation and Paige West for their generous support in the funding of this book.

"Brain Madras" and "Haywire Will" were written in response to two paintings by Jonathan Lasker and originally appeared in *Queen Street Quarterly*. Thank you J.L.

"Hoe Wind" and "Morning Kitchen" originally appeared in *The Hat*. I would like to thank the editors of these journals.

I wish to gratefully acknowledge Cory Reynolds for her continued love and support.

I would also like to thank Paige West for her generosity.

Jacket image by Chéri Samba, 1978. Courtesy of J.A. Patras, Paris.

Designed by Bryan McHugh.

Distributed by SPD, Berkeley, CA.
Left Hand Books website: lefthandbooks.com

ISBN 1-880516-28-4

Manufactured in the United States of America.

Contents

Morning Kitchen	3
On In	4
An Archivist	5
Brain Madras	6
Photaffair	7
Now I Know	8
Horizon's Handouts	9
Broadcast	10
Left Right	11
Weird Mutiny	12
All That I Bring	13
Toes See	14
Other Than You	15
To the Cast of a Play within a Film	16
Heart Gong	17
Whale	18
Two-eared Auditorium	19
Mid	21
Hoe Wind	22
Yellow You	23
Post-Inkblot	24
Mr. Magoo-ish	25
Make Me	26
Rain Drama	27
Carpenter's Risk	28
Grotesque Work	29
Haywire Will	30
Generic Span	31
No Sweater	32
On Break	34
Fork Future	35
A Colloid	36

Counterweight	37
Walk through Me	38
Armature Air	39
Let's Not Be Said	40
Pump	41
Marry Me City	42
A Long Heart	43
What on Earth Is He Made Of?	49
Stoic Squash	50
Dashboard	51
Oh Boy	52
Cobbled Side	53
Things	54
Glaring Forest	56
To Date	57
Hibernation	59
Two-faced	60
Puddle	61
Divisions	62
Bull's Eye	63
Steeplechase	64
Fruit	65
Grid Sea	66
The Same Day	67
Nocturne	68
Kettle	69
Turn on Him	70

Mallet Eyes

Morning Kitchen

A city of cinema leaf
comes to light

a director's cut of
green now playing

at the end
of every
stem

Just green,
no trailers
to be
seen

On In

to a day away
from one so different
I assemble the news
numbers look nappy
crowding the phone
on to something of their own
(and with their own kind)
I don't mind
yet one day away
I may

An Archivist

Well-proportioned
after erosion

with blockhead held
by bunglecord

with memory cubbied
on the osseous
shelves of an archive
of odd feelings

An archivist walks out
this arm of sand

and shakes the ocean's hand

Brain Madras

Light on the wall
morning's dull saw

Multifaceted memories
cut to a tie

and I, here

in this convulsing canopy

am patched
like brain madras

seedlings sprouting into
strangletrees
strange as I squeeze

all of what I
consider most

Photaffair

How long
till low
gas gurgle

how long
till the
appalling
halt how

long can
your string
necklace

bridge the
hike of
my like

how long
will that
stone rock

its cribless
kind

Now I Know

there is wind
so still

breeze so flat

turbulence
so dead

now I know

there is a point
between here and

near the still, flat
dead of you

beside the night sea

off the shore of me

Horizon's Handouts

I can see far from here
to days down there

that passed, each fast
each at a time

bottlenecking the horizon
waiting for handouts

I recall how that one
got out of a bind
like a contortionist

and that empty
and scrawny one

how it tried to
stir brickcrumbs
how it tried to
move shambles

Broadcast

I can hear for the dune
but so did the ocean
diagonal upon it
by noon

and radio waves
revolve the berm
of my attention

back to the conveyor
of cotton with cap-
sized clouds and

a gray-striped wind…
for which I have
no receipt

Left Right

Left wrong
bottom right

black descending
a Siamese branch

to a thespian skull
with tooth canals

by now stained
like freakish bark

from years bingeing
on dark

Weird Mutiny

Deep-fried frown
golden crisp moral

in a way I feel abnormal
so I meander

into the mote
of my own
emotions

and drown…

and tattling kids
come down

and lift this log
of saturation and
immaturation

and carve a canoe
to row in mutiny

and hoist me and
beach me to shore

and flame hot booze me
with folklore

All That I Bring

Buried in shame
the grass wags
and pigeons practice
Impressionism in their
lofts and perspiring in
a tree a bag can see
through itself at me
and all that I bring
and one other thing

Toes See

Down as
me

on the
amount

of it

lids
close

on the
surround

of it

twenty blocks
from knee

only toes
see

Other Than You

Do you detect it
in me

        as you flee? If so

I understand, I know

how the blur
wants the drop

        to blur. I prefer

your dyed indifference
to an intensely centered
thing of thought, so

        understand, while

I expand
with the sun
over day, that I may too

engage a few

To the Cast of a Play within a Film

Near the ear
losing grip
sopping the sip

of applause gulping
because quaking

clasp holler
over collar brooming
my boots to

the flesh circuitry
of your lips to

where a crow sits
perched like a boom
over the upholstered sky

I can feel this twitch
near my heart niche

as I gauge every
feathery tilt of your
soar and as I store

the rattle of what
doesn't settle…

I'm your lathe

Heart Gong

On an engine
for one dark
I embark

over your salt
swimming hair

the fare
just to stare

and think
for the thought
to tantalize

and hear
for your gong
song rise…

your mallet eyes

Whale

Doubt
with
the
dive
I've
made
sleek
to
see
the
craburetor
on
its
back
closing
my
swallow
of
the
sun
and
the
moon
a
whale
with
a
school
of
apprehension

Two-eared Auditorium

1.
Getting loud with this contemplative scroll—
the montage of me—the mind's mysterious
corm—I can feel its spine fray quite
lightly, but when I squint the world
double, I see a crude crack in its head
and unsealed envelopes across its eyes.
Your journey was so far its start was
getting there; berated by storms of all
kinds, flashed by backlit cloud forms,
dissolved into roadmist as if by a
chemist. All of this so that a single
drop, the size of her first pierced ear,
could be viewed rupturing into five
marooned prisms—each the point of a
pyramid as I ascend with the other
birds of this handful flock into this
aggressive sky, stabbing at us with
swords of shine, snorting and cutting its
fifth line—clouds like nervous secretaries
unable to collate themselves—
the rusty sun making an awful
exit for the so-called radiant one.

2.
All of your faces form a stencil
for the spraying of an accidental
speech. A wave lifts its hem then
becoming the tube of what's perpetually
new. Let's meet before the present is a
crash. Let's meet before memory soaks
our socks. A millimeter is still
talking its big game of mileage.
A slate-toothed turret shows the
shade's rash, drifting out over sedan
sediment and further. When will I
feel the staple which just bent
across the last page I lived?—age
becoming violent.... The bridge, how it
bends in arching bound for no
reason—its semi-shadow with under-
water support—its left-for-dead—
its doggy-paddlers.... "Think!" says the
height of my head, as I head across,
"think on your feet!" which I
do, deciding that this bridge is only
for two of the sides.

Mid

A barge
a tug
from
the

harbor

I was asked
to take a
step

outside

urged, teased
toward
the

gutterloaf

of compost
leaf

to be the
star
of
a

carcass
fountain

Hoe Wind

"Great intellects guess well."
—Edgar Allan Poe

The hoe wind
again here it is

panting. I heard it
burrow what's beneath

and drag the waves
as if they were joints

I'm brighter today
ya know man, I've
been seen with Skavoovie

kids unkept and hep
and this scale enlarging
as if my heart were an egg

and you were a chicken

collecting nuts in your cape

Yellow You

Too asleep
to snore

pre-dew
I've left
for you

owning the
road I got
on sooner

ahead of
a humid
day with

its tacky
sunrise
display

past Philthi
boarded-up
Baltimore

I've left
not for you

but for you

Post-Inkblot

Entirely not
an inkblot

(despite the family resemblance)

I thought I was wasting my time
when it sank like a bunkbed how

now is asleep
slung on a train

and without a
message at all

sprayed spread-eagle

on the side
of that mall

Mr. Magoo-ish

The clock counts its
fingers and muscles

moor to the pier
of my back

and then the oblivion
calculates

its ancient
conundrum

and presses C
counting on me

to clear, but
first to live all

that can link

which is perfect
'cause I'm
Mr. Magoo-ish

I think

Make Me

harsh as day
or woozy as night
but make me not
the needy light
pestering the
transition along
both right
and wrong

Rain Drama

Will the rain
knock me down
hard as it falls
or with walls
of wet will it set
me in a seat
and it on a set
the curtain aside
where I hide

Carpenter's Risk

A
bench
sits

with a
cane

and a
house
leans

on old
tall grass

and all
the squares

in toolbox
basements

count their
metrical
blessings

Grotesque Work

Pecking hands
of a surgeon

tired lips
of a smile

cement stare
at grass grotesque

work glazing
the glance of
a plain day

pecking birds
fly away…wings

unwinding wind
an ease given
to that same
bothered bill….

Who wants to fly
after the thinking
of such sky?

Haywire Will

Each time I try to reach
the haywire of my will

I find only primary wonders—
pale green becoming the wash
of my whitewater urge. Numbers?

They bailed! Grammar got gaunt
yet what goes will come

out again for a jaunt

sidestreets are my ribs

Generic Span

Clear rain cellophane
a zip-locked second

nerves like weeds
with little hold

in the cracks
between hours

should I sip from
what comes high
to consume the sun

or toejack down
this elevation
of oddness

and accept the
how of being leashed

below the birds

No Sweater

Hey I love your clogs
why should I lace you
there's a way the shapes
remain composed if not
withheld your window
(should I throw this)
could be anywhere from
the pebbled behindness of
blindness how the
manual clicking of your
circulature melds with
the fragments of a clock
enamored as you are
by the open vault of
your own brain with
its multi-electricities the
full spectrum of color
begins to gray grey begins
to play all we've wanted
to say just walked away
hiking this slow ramp
up to me words want
in but are denied as
I have been from the
branches that squirrel seems
to be enjoying at least
the cabs are of dirty
yellow loud all night
for which I applaud it
If I could hold you
I'd pat the broad coat
of your sweater all four

of our elbows are gone
anyway

On Break

with this ambiguous shape

my bare feet
can they steer

can they care

for what I hear

sitting space
each hair

asleep sleepy
chair

knowing you
may be too

narrow…oh

Fork Future

Moon bombs the bald
between hair

youth off yearning
off needling
another

hard-look hills
have come flat
(not steep)

and dreams
have arrived
half-asleep

So why not a dream
unmemorable and modestly
a rival to all the
convenience of all
the experience?

A Colloid

To my family-tumbling tide, I'd
like to mention with intervention
that I'm distinctly alone

mixing
a colloid
less breathable
than air

more new than this year's flu
(I haven't a clue)

but gripped by the mad boil
of a test tube ton,
errands
I run and run

wishing it were as it was when we were
boys

looping from
diving to ladder
the water so warmer
I'm in it like a tanker

'cause otherwise it won't move slow

Counterweight

Night came
to have its way
here empty
as I lay

it took a cheek
in my mandible
wide with expectation

phosphorescent face
are you along like a fish
glowing through the deep bay

of tomorrow's early day

with this secret
near my spleen
I'm beyond a lean

I'm a
downside-

up "u"

an "n"

Walk through Me

Tired of it

crushed springs
beg for pardon

plead for full extension and of my body anything

but the deal
for deep distance

sleep's insistence

on the engine
of evening beyond
the arch of dark

Armature Air

Between work
I walk

between ears
a nose

and the between
I haven't seen…

your eyes are the size
of quarters for one
born to dimes

two skillets they burn
like empty iron

while I disassemble
my stare into
multiple peeks

and while
I instruct
the air

to stand
before you

to court you

till the next time I see you

Let's Not Be Said

Green bones
in orange hips

chic
I sip

green
orange each
so lonely
a reach

so no
matter
graphics

let's not
be pictorial

listen!

let's not
be said

Pump

Vaguely up close
to your evening
emerald

vaguely made hollow
by the dilation
of your flirtation

gallon over gallon
you're a pump of
exuberance

a white-bearded pump

Marry Me City

Marry me to
your periphery
of inserted coast

as that theater
becomes a corner

inform me of
the order put
in by that trader

and those holed
up old upstairs
uptown

slip into my
sub-unconscious
and my unsung
conscience

slip this ring
on my finger

so that we may be
together while

the L turns
to a cool summer

seat and suburbs
remain the brunt
of all our jokes

A Long Heart

Not
one
day
but
so
gradual
to
be
called
never
Two
faces
in
winter's
whiskered
hourglass
two
skin
suits
of
scar
in
the
clutch
of
a
start
it
was
time
we
part

Had
thought
inflated
the
light
bouncing
it
a
bit
closer
to
evening
stretching
it
a
bit
thinner
over
dinner
Would
the
adjacent
inside
have
any
blue
and
yellow
after
all
the
cobalt
skulls
had
been

smashed
I
could
relish
in
purple
pomegranate
saturation
so
why
do
I
keep
hauling
this
green
cadaver
so
far
from
its
origin
Your
face
keeps
getting
saltier
sucked
back
into
your
pores
puppies
I
imagine

grabbed
by
their
bellybags
and
rush-dropped
into
the
eyes
they
came
from
I
soothe
you
all
day
with
the
song
of
owls
iron
steam
dripping
into
water
coffee
a
dry
mugloop
And
work
works
about

as
well
as
the
daily
stack
of
sound
played
through
like
45s
Pinned
by
knees
the
held-down
heart
has
been
delegated
to
the
field
and
how
we
wish
for
its
return
how
we
wish
for

it
to
swing
open
its
spiral
pad
and
show
us
its
notes

What on Earth Is He Made Of?

asked the perfect flames
devouring it like corn-on-the-cob
the lens had been buttered

the smoke was a lavender vein
the trees were far from yellow
just alone sat this acreage

splinters in wool I thought
of those stick arms
perfect for crows (less so
for arrows) proud limb

like wires for draping
shadowy corners and
then he was built:
a model in my ear

and I switched in my chair
more a log-figure than he
whittled by city-goers

mowed down by adult boulders
staring into diluted amber tarns

Stoic Squash

Little the green
can do with
such gray

May and

like a nun
on the can
it sits

its wart
hidden

from view

Dashboard

He figured

best as
odd digits

access even
numbers

that finger-counting
would be his means

and that wind
was a pretty
good excuse

for loss

Oh Boy

"That ain't right"
—George Jones

Sun pleats
of tunic sky

on the road
shadows lie

silver card
dealin' silver
card a

hard hand
of clouds
to ignore

car-deep
yellin' jeep
beep beep

steerin' man
forearm tan
throwin' my can

Cobbled Side

Shifting to its
submerged knee

the outer sea
hasn't hills
for errands

the fuse was
just thrown but
there is no
current nor

is there a
moment

and though we
have set down
and set up shop

the land may still
not recline on
its cobbled side

to be studied

Things

My mind was in a spin
I just hadn't put the needle
down

the tilt of her head
teased the horizon toward
a clockwise condition

isn't it rare to find
a circle truly owned by
a spiral and why

can't we circles just touch
and not overlap so much

the tree out the kitchen
seems straighter I think
it has improved its posture

is this thought warm
or is it frozen as
winter television it

appears that there is nothing
but aluminum-sided silos
and popped wheelies away

from where the streets seem
to wind with my escorted
whims

and still I'm riding the brake

near the outermost reach of
the ambiance of emptiness

county roads like fingernail marks

Glaring Forest

Indifferent to
a moon-lit leader

Indifferent to
the bone-shoulder short of dying

Indifferent to
the poor sofa porch

Indifferent forest
with your torch

To Date

When I
yawn

and I'm
bound

to the
lawn

blue wrists
behind

my back
and

the moon
disrobes

the trees
alerting

me to
well

up with
the

sadness of
summer

so late
the

moon missing
dew

to date

Hibernation

To conserve you
I shut my eyes
to you

though lies
to tell of
hibernation

will open
and stand before you

like 2 black bears

in ape costumes

Two-faced

Tottering the
walk is a
spool

the rain is
a prickly tool

while your
in school

hob-nobbin'
with the window's

two-faced wind

Puddle

I'm ice-fishing

in your circles
and it's bitter

back to where
warmth disintegrated

and—hey!—was that
just a nibble?

I could swear I felt something and I'm unspooling

and colossal is
the solid sea

and when it thaws
our love will stand

in a puddle

Divisions

Gaps of
fall sky

follow the
bird fly

thrown sand
a band of

trees stand
a crowd
a cloud

and the
rest of
the top

of the
turnpike

and a toll

and the roll

Bull's Eye

Under thunder
my face is blinking

under ink flows
my inkling and

here is bull's eye
for the aim of
my thinking

the valve is off
to release my
reasoning

that I build
from my feet
with crete

pour this floor
before the street

flow into
what they'll never know into

slow as the sun takes the moon's shift

Steeplechase

It was rising up me
like a flame in my
neck when the thought
of you combusted in
my brain

and it wasn't pretty
tossing pillows to new
positions as if I
were a storm

here you are on the
relief of my plastic

rubbed over my
overly defined
quirks

and tissue-blotted business…

and here they come
winning words
over my gate

and a few jockeys
down

on paper

Fruit

Let me live
in your visceral
clock

outstretched in your peripheral stock

resting unloaded
on your loading
dock

in and out
of a nap

details
in the dirt
of this map

that we'll use
to find this day

again and when

all that is
new has
become known

forgetting will
be fruit

Grid Sea

Only out in
the grid sea

only from me

and I haven't
ID to operate
the current

nor can I
rip the tides
like *Times* articles
worth saving

no longer nor ever
do I use peyote

so you're gone

only out in
the grid sea

gone from me

The Same Day

> *"One can speak of the good mental health of Van Gogh, who in his whole life, cooked only one of his hands and did nothing else except once to cut off his left ear,..."*
> —*Antonin Artaud*

Neither house
nor hut

just the gut

the shell
never meant
to cover
the nut
but

the greatest place to be

in this
day which
in a way

you
gave
me

high-fiving
and whispering

in my internal
ear "you take it from here"

Nocturne

Wrap every star
in your paper
thin eyes

urge even night

away

for so luminous
is your skin

Kettle

Summer's off its burner

and the kettle of brain
just jellied

puppies have a claim to dog youth
don't you think

most of me
has just been led inside
and the open wide

is a hand-me-down

Turn on Him

Dinged were the
fenders of his
charging vision

musethings having
been plucked from
unbathed eagle wings

the door parted
like Philip Johnson's
glass gown but

they all remained
too mod for mime
the monocle was

no longer acting
in its epic of
pre-sand scenario

no it wasn't looking
good for this flash-
lit day hit the

sun clung as if
it were mooshed
mud on his chicken

wire nerves
though his pond was
rushing for the first

time in years it
seemed to be gripping
the hair of a fallen

tree that once stood
erect like a tall
fourth-grader in a class

picture a rock off
the dock I smack
black water knowing I'll

skip out a ways
and then with oars
I skim away the

residue of missions past
my horn drowned out
by the coded cry of

tankers and there
in the distortion
the expression

it's my own